YOUNG, FEARLESS, AWESOME

THE ILLUSTRATORS

Andy Shaw

Andy lives in New Zealand. His illustration journey peaked at the age of five when he effortlessly drew a self-portrait that featured long, striped rainbow arms. He spent the next thirty-one years trying to re-create that feeling.

Anna Higgie

Anna is an Australian-born illustrator now living and working in Bristol, England. She spends most of her time in her studio, where she uses a combination of traditional and digital techniques to create her illustrations.

Anna Stiles

London-born Anna studied French at college before becoming an illustrator in 2009. Anna makes detail-rich, hand-drawn illustrations and is especially interested in detail and mark making. She works mostly in ink and paint.

Jessica Singh

Jessica is from Australia and is a graduate of Central Saint Martins in London. Inspired by her Indian heritage, she loves vibrant color and traditional textile designs. When she's not drawing, Jessica loves traveling, walking in nature, and collecting crystals.

Kelly Thompson

After an initial career in fashion photography, Kelly began to capture her subjects as ephemeral illustrations. As a freelance artist, Kelly first works by hand, sketching in pencil, before using Photoshop and adding color with help from her trusty Wacom.

Sofia Bonati

Born in Argentina, Sofia now lives in the UK. She first studied geology before completing a degree in graphic design and illustration. She likes to add inks, watercolor, and gouache to her soft pencil drawings—making her portraits elegant and refined.

Text, design, and illustration © Welbeck Children's Limited 2020

All rights reserved. Published by B.E.S Publishing

All inquiries should be addressed to:
Peterson's Publishing, LLC
8740 Lucent Blvd, Ste 400
Highlands Ranch, CO 80129
www.petersonsbooks.com

Published by arrangement with Welbeck Children's Limited,
an imprint of the Welbeck Publishing Group.

ISBN: 978-1-4380-8909-6

10 9 8 7 6 5 4 3 2 1

Printed in Heshan, China

First edition, April 2020

YOUNG, FEARLESS, AWESOME

TWENTY-FIVE YOUNG PEOPLE
WHO CHANGED THE WORLD

CONTENTS

Introduction *6*

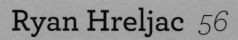 

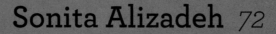

Introduction

Kids are too young to make a difference, right? Wrong! Get ready to meet twenty-five young people who never let their age hold them back.

Your ideas might be small, but that doesn't mean they can't grow (like you). Nine-year-old **Felix Finkbeiner** planted one tree to help the planet—and now there are fourteen billion in his name. Of course, Felix couldn't do all that by himself. He inspired other people to get involved, too. Perhaps your parents aren't on board with your vision? Six-year-old **Ryan Hreljac** did months of housework to convince his parents to support him in raising money to build wells in Africa.

These kids refused to be held back by other people's expectations. **Victoria Arlen** was told she would never walk again, but she defied the doctors. And fifteen-year-old **Sunakali Budha** challenged the conventions of her remote Nepalese community to follow her soccer dreams.

Some of these children had horrific experiences, but they took positive action. Four-year-old **Alexandra Scott** had cancer, but she raised money with a lemonade stand to fund research that would help other children suffering from the disease.

When these young people saw something wrong, they didn't wait for the adults to do something. They just did it themselves. Just like fifteen-year-old **Claudette Colvin**. In 1955, she stood up against racial segregation in the South. Today, **Emma González** campaigns for stricter laws on gun control. And then there's **Thandiwe Chama**, who has been fighting to improve education for all children since she was eight.

When it comes to changing people's attitudes, how you communicate is important. **George the Poet** uses rhyme and rhythm to speak up about the injustice he sees, and sixteen-year-old **Sonita Alizadeh** makes rap videos to protest against child marriage. **Anne Frank** couldn't speak out during her short lifetime, but she wrote an inspirational diary that has since been read by millions.

But don't worry if you don't always know what to say. Ten-year-old **Samantha Smith** didn't have the answers, so she asked questions. And in doing so, she brought people together across the divide of the Cold War.

Of course, it's not always about changing the world. Whether an athlete, a world-record breaker, an inventor, an environmentalist, a writer, a fundraiser, a campaigner, a poet, or a ballet dancer, these kids all have one thing in common: they all pushed themselves to be their best.

We've tried to imagine what the twenty-five young achievers in this book might do in the kind of situations you could find yourself in, though of course we can only guess at the advice they might give you. So along with their stories, you can read about what **Malala Yousafzai** might advise if you don't see eye to eye with your parents, or what **Greta Thunberg** might suggest for helping the planet.

Now turn the page, start reading . . .
and be awesome and fearless!

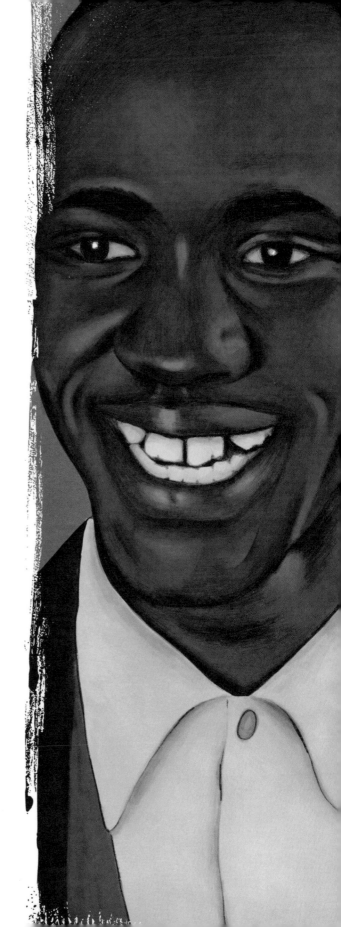

ANNE FRANK

EXTRAORDINARY DIARIST

In many ways, Anne Frank was an ordinary girl. She liked going to the beach, she was a chatterbox, and she could be quite sassy. But Anne was Jewish, living in dangerous times. When her family was forced to hide from the Nazis, she turned to writing in her diary. The result was one of the world's most famous books.

NAME: *Annelies Marie Frank*

BORN: June 12, 1929   DIED: February or March 1945 (age fifteen)

NATIONALITY: German

ROLE: Diarist who became a symbol of the Holocaust

Anne Frank was born to a Jewish family in the German city of Frankfurt. Her parents were Edith and Otto, and she had an older sister named Margot.

In 1933, Adolf Hitler's Nazi Party came to power. They unjustly blamed Jewish people for Germany's problems and began making life very difficult for them. Anne's parents decided to move the family to safety, choosing Amsterdam in the Netherlands.

Anne and Margot learned Dutch and went to school. Anne was known for her lively nature and for being a chatterbox! She loved reading, riding her bike, and playing with her many friends.

When Anne was ten, Germany invaded Poland, marking the start of the Second World War. A year later, Germany invaded the Netherlands. Gradually, life became very difficult for Jewish people there, too. They weren't allowed to own businesses, go to the movie theater, or walk in parks. Jewish children were forced to attend special schools.

On her thirteenth birthday, Anne received a diary as a present. In her first entry, on June 12, 1942, she addressed an imaginary friend named Kitty and wrote, "I hope I will be able to confide everything to you . . . ."

By now, things were getting really bad for Jewish people, and they were forced to wear a yellow Star of David sewn onto their clothes. That summer, Margot received a letter summoning her to a "work" camp. Realizing there was no time to lose, Otto moved his family into a secret hiding place that he had been preparing.

The secret annex was a cramped set of rooms next to Otto's place of work. Its entrance was a door hidden behind a bookcase. Six of Otto's friends and colleagues agreed to help the Franks, at great risk to their own lives. Before long, another Jewish family—Mr. and Mrs. van Pels and their fifteen-year-old son, Peter—moved into the annex, later followed by a dentist named Fritz Pfeffer.

Anne recorded her feelings in her diary. Addressing each entry to Kitty, she wrote beautifully about her hopes, her frustrations, and her fears. We can only imagine what it was like for lively Anne being cooped up, fearful of making any sound. Writing was her escape. Like many teenage girls, she clashed with her parents, thought about boys, and felt angst and loneliness. She also wrote about her dream of becoming a famous writer.

The group had been in hiding for nearly two years when, on August 4, 1944, the German state police stormed the annex. The families were transported to the Auschwitz concentration camp. Anne and Margot were then sent on to the Bergen-Belsen camp, where they both died from illness.

Otto was the group's only survivor. When he returned to Amsterdam, Miep Gies—one of the people who had helped the family in hiding—gave Otto Anne's diary, which she had discovered on the annex floor.

Anne's diary was first published in 1947 and has since been translated into more than seventy languages and been read by tens of millions of people. *The Diary of a Young Girl* is an important record of the Holocaust, but also a heartbreaking testament to Anne's extraordinary spirit.

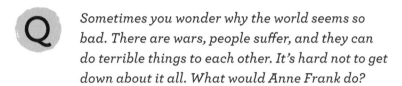

BE FEARLESS, LIKE ANNE FRANK!

Q *Sometimes you wonder why the world seems so bad. There are wars, people suffer, and they can do terrible things to each other. It's hard not to get down about it all. What would Anne Frank do?*

A Anne was alive at a time when the Nazis put Jewish people through dreadful suffering. But despite the tragedy that surrounded her, she managed to find flashes of hope in the darkness. She wrote, "I don't think of all the misery but of the beauty that still remains." Perhaps that's what she'd tell you, too. Keep hoping and remember that plenty of wonderful things happen in the world, too.

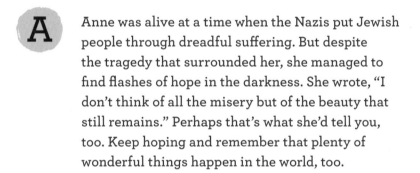

In spite of everything, I still believe people are good at heart.

ANNE FRANK

CLAUDETTE COLVIN

CIVIL RIGHTS HEROINE

You've heard of civil rights icon Rosa Parks, right? She became famous after being arrested in 1955 for refusing to give up her bus seat to a white man. But did you know that just nine months earlier, fifteen-year-old Claudette Colvin was arrested for exactly the same "crime?" While Rosa Parks became a powerful symbol of America's civil rights movement, Claudette's bravery has largely been forgotten.

NAME: *Claudette Colvin*

BORN: September 5, 1939

NATIONALITY: American

ROLE: Civil rights pioneer

Born in Alabama, in the Deep South, Claudette Colvin grew up at a time when there was racial segregation. This meant that African Americans were treated as second-class citizens. They had different schools, churches, and stores from white people, and they had to put up with signs that said things like "Whites Only" and "Colored Must Sit in Rear."

Claudette saw first-hand the ugly racism that was commonplace in the South at the time. It affected all aspects of life. She remembers how, when she needed school shoes, her mother had to trace the outline of her foot onto a paper bag to get her shoe size because she wasn't allowed to try the shoes on in the store.

At her segregated school, Claudette was a bright student who was also rather rebellious. She worked hard but shocked her classmates by refusing to straighten her hair—as was expected of black people at the time. In class, she learned about black history. The experiences of Harriet Tubman and Sojourner Truth, who both escaped slavery and became political activists, made a deep impression on her.

On March 2, 1955, Claudette and her friends decided to take the bus home from school. When a young white woman boarded the full bus, the driver asked the girls to give her a seat. Although three of them stood up, Claudette did not—she told the driver she had paid her fare and it was her constitutional right to remain seated. Although there was now a seat for the white woman, she still wouldn't sit down because that would have meant sitting in the same row as a black person.

Claudette later said that she felt like, *"Sojourner Truth was pushing down on one shoulder and Harriet Tubman was pushing down on the other, saying, 'Sit down girl!'"* The teenager was roughly taken off the bus by two police officers, placed in an adult prison, and charged with defying segregation laws. Claudette's story was reported locally, and at first she was seen as someone who could become the "face" of the civil rights movement. But it was decided she was perhaps too young, and when she later became pregnant, her story faded into the background.

Nine months later, Rosa Parks made a similar stand, refusing to give up her bus seat for a white passenger. This time, though, the act of defiance was reported around the world. Parks's action sparked the Montgomery bus boycott—when many black people refused to travel on the city buses for 381 days.

In 1956, Claudette and three other women filed a lawsuit against the city of Montgomery. It was called *Browder v. Gayle,* and eventually the Supreme Court ruled that segregation on buses must end. It was a huge victory for civil rights.

Claudette later became a nurse in New York City, but she didn't tell many people about her story. In 2009, a book—*Claudette Colvin*—was published, and it shone a spotlight on her actions. Although Rosa Parks is the name that people celebrate when it comes to the civil rights movement, the book finally gave Claudette some of the credit she deserves.

BE FEARLESS, LIKE CLAUDETTE COLVIN!

Q *You're with some classmates when some of them start taunting a girl who has recently arrived from another country. You feel sorry for the new student —she's struggling to fit in and obviously in need of a friend—but you don't want to draw attention to yourself. What might Claudette Colvin do?*

A Claudette Colvin knew very well what it's like to live in an unfair society. It would have been very easy for her to play it safe, but she knew the system wasn't right. That sense of injustice gave her the courage to make a stand. We can't know for sure what she'd tell you, but she would probably encourage you to stand up for what you know is right and make the new girl feel welcome. And who knows—you might make a great new friend!

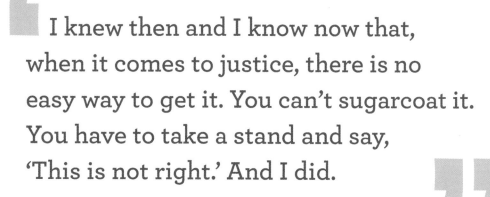

"I knew then and I know now that, when it comes to justice, there is no easy way to get it. You can't sugarcoat it. You have to take a stand and say, 'This is not right.' And I did."

CLAUDETTE COLVIN

KIM SOO-NYUNG

ASTONISHING ARCHER

Archer Kim Soo-Nyung wasn't nicknamed "Viper" for nothing. At the age of seventeen, her incredible eye and killer strike made her a double gold medalist at the 1988 Summer Olympics in Seoul, and she went on to dominate her sport. After several years in retirement, Kim decided she wasn't quite finished with archery yet, and she made an incredible comeback at the 2000 Summer Olympics in Sydney.

NAME: **Kim Soo-Nyung**

BORN: April 5, 1971

NATIONALITY: South Korean

ROLE: Olympic gold-medalist and world-champion archer

Kim Soo-Nyung was born in the province of Chungcheongbuk-do in South Korea. When she was nine years old, a teacher recommended archery to her as an after-school activity. The teacher later said that she had thought Kim would do well at the sport because she was taller than average and had long arms.

The teacher turned out to be right—Kim was a natural! From the age of thirteen, Kim decided to put all her effort into the sport, often neglecting her school studies (not generally something to be recommended, though it paid off in this case!).

In 1987, Kim set a world record at thirty meters and was selected for her national team. At the 1988 Olympic Games—held in the South Korean capital, Seoul—the seventeen-year-old really hit the mark. In the individual event, she took the gold medal with a strong lead of twelve points. Her teammates, ages seventeen and eighteen, took silver and bronze. The three youngsters won gold in the women's team event, making Kim a double gold medalist.

Following her amazing success, Kim won consecutive World Archery Championships in 1989 and 1991. Her strike was so terrifyingly accurate that one of her coaches started calling her "Viper," and the nickname stuck. Kim held almost every record, including for the distances of seventy, sixty, fifty, and thirty meters.

At the 1992 Barcelona Olympics, Kim lost out on the individual gold medal to her teammate Cho Youn-Jeon by seven points, but she and her teammates won the women's team gold. Kim now had three Olympic golds and a silver.

Kim retired from the sport to raise children. In 1999, when she was twenty-eight, an archery manufacturer asked her to do some publicity work and she felt inspired to return to archery.

Shooting accurately was harder for Kim than she'd imagined it would be, but after a national competition she felt the old fire returning. After several months of intense training, she was back on the Olympic team and headed for the 2000 games in Sydney. Take that for a comeback!

Kim put in an amazing performance at the Sydney Olympics and was just two arrows from the final—but she lost to her teammate, Yun Mi-Jin, who took the gold. Kim won the bronze medal.

Two days later, the Korean women's team won each of their matches with ease. It was the fourth gold medal for Kim, making her the most successful Korean archer of all time. Her reputation was sealed when, in 2011, the International Archery Federation named her Female Archer of the Twentieth Century.

BE FEARLESS, LIKE KIM SOO-NYUNG!

Q *You were pretty good at basketball in grade school, but then other stuff came up and you lost interest. Lately, you've wanted to get more exercise and your mom suggested basketball—but it's been years and the other girls will be so much better than you. What's the point?*

A Kim didn't even pick up an archer's bow during her six years off, but it didn't take her long to find her mojo. Sure, she was out of practice, but she was determined. She'd most likely suggest you throw yourself back in. You might not be as good as the others —for now—but they'd better watch out!

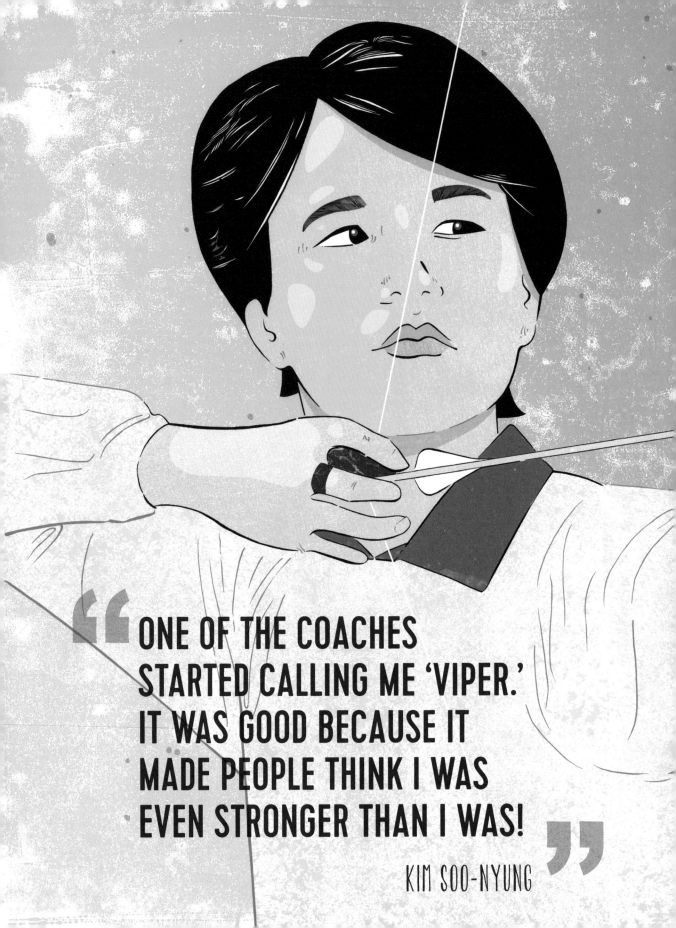

"ONE OF THE COACHES STARTED CALLING ME 'VIPER.' IT WAS GOOD BECAUSE IT MADE PEOPLE THINK I WAS EVEN STRONGER THAN I WAS!"

KIM SOO-NYUNG

RYAN WHITE

BRAVE AIDS ACTIVIST

At the age of thirteen, Ryan White was
diagnosed with AIDS and given just
six months to live. He wasn't ready to give
up on life though, and he wanted to return
to school. However, people were afraid of
catching AIDS from him, so he was met
with fear and hatred. Ryan bravely fought
against this discrimination and ignorance
for the rest of his short life, opening
hearts and changing attitudes.

BORN: December 6, 1971   DIED: April 8, 1990 (age eighteen)

NATIONALITY: American

ROLE: AIDS spokesperson and activist

• •

Ryan White was born in Kokomo, Indiana. When he was three days old, doctors told his parents that he had hemophilia. This condition means that a person's blood doesn't clot properly, so even the tiniest scratch can be life-threatening.

Ryan's family was given hope with a new treatment called Factor VII. It was made from donated blood, and doctors hoped it would allow hemophiliacs to lead normal lives. Ryan's parents didn't hesitate to agree to the treatment.

Growing up, Ryan managed to keep his hemophilia hidden from his classmates, but as he approached his thirteenth birthday, he began to feel really sick and was very tired all the time. Eventually pneumonia was diagnosed, and Ryan's parents learned their son had AIDS (Acquired Immunodeficiency Syndrome).

Ryan received his diagnosis at a time when many people didn't really understand AIDS or how it was spread. AIDS is caused by the HIV virus and Ryan developed the disease because he was treated with blood from an infected donor.

Doctors gave Ryan just six months to live, but he didn't want to dwell on that. Instead, he hoped for a normal life, to go to school, and see his friends. However, he could never have imagined the fear and hatred he would meet. Even though it was now known that AIDS could not be spread through casual contact, like touching, people were still afraid of Ryan. And his school was determined to keep him out.

Ryan's family filed a lawsuit and eventually won the case. He was allowed to return to school, but things were still really difficult for him. He had to use a separate toilet and disposable silverware. Children were cruel to him, taunting him about being gay—AIDS was often called the "gay plague" because people believed it mainly afflicted the gay community. Some parents even took their children out of the school.

Eventually Ryan's family moved away from Kokomo to nearby Cicero, where they were made to feel welcome. On Ryan's first day at his new school, the principal and several children shook his hand. Meanwhile, the story had been picked up by the media and Ryan began to receive support from celebrities around the world, such as singer Elton John and former president Ronald Reagan. Ryan soon became the "face" of AIDS, discussing his condition on TV, appearing in newspaper articles, and taking part in educational campaigns.

By 1990, Ryan's health was deteriorating rapidly and he died just one month before he was due to graduate from high school. A few months later, a bill called the Ryan White CARE Act was passed into law. It provides funds to support the diagnosis and treatment of AIDS.

Instead of being a victim, Ryan chose to stand up against the hatred he saw around him. Realizing that hatred often comes from ignorance and fear, he made it his mission to educate people and change attitudes toward AIDS.

BE FEARLESS, LIKE RYAN WHITE!

Q *There's a refugee at school with a facial disfigurement. You've heard other children laughing behind her back, and you know it's not right. What would Ryan White do?*

A Despite his hemophilia and AIDS diagnosis, Ryan White just wanted to be treated like a regular kid. He knew how painful it was to encounter prejudice, and he'd probably encourage you to speak up and tell people that it's just not acceptable to taunt someone because they're different in some way. And he'd encourage you to befriend the girl and let her know she's welcome in your school.

> "Because of the lack of education on AIDS, fear, panic, and lies surrounded me."
>
> RYAN WHITE

SAMANTHA SMITH

AMBASSADOR OF PEACE

Samantha Smith grew up at a time when
the threat of nuclear war between the
United States and the Soviet Union terrified
people. So she decided to take her worries
straight to the top. She wrote to the Soviet
leader asking, *"Why do you want to conquer
the world?"* Amazingly, he replied—AND
he invited her to visit the Soviet Union!
Samantha discovered that Soviet children
were just like American children—and
became an ambassador for peace.

NAME: *Samantha Smith*

BORN: June 29, 1972 DIED: August 25, 1985 (age thirteen)
NATIONALITY: American
ROLE: Peace ambassador and child actress

The Cold War era ran from the end of the Second World War in 1945 until 1991. During this time, there was a lot of tension between the United States and the Soviet Union, and the threat of nuclear war was very real.

In 1983, when Samantha Smith was ten years old, she asked her mother if there was going to be a nuclear war. Her mother showed her a photograph of Yuri Andropov (the leader of the Soviet Union) on the cover of *Time* magazine and suggested Samantha ask him that in a letter.

So Samantha did just that. She wrote, *"I have been worrying about Russia and the United States getting into a nuclear war . . . . Why do you want to conquer the world or at least our country?"*

Samantha didn't get an immediate response, but her letter was published in the Soviet newspaper *Pravda*. She wrote a second letter, this time to the Soviet Embassy in Washington, D.C., asking why Andropov hadn't responded. His answer arrived just over a week later.

Andropov told Samantha that she was courageous, and she reminded him of Becky in the book *Huckleberry Finn* by Mark Twain. He insisted that they didn't want to use nuclear weapons. He wrote, "We want peace for ourselves and for all peoples of the planet." He finished by inviting Samantha to visit.

So, in the summer of 1983, the Smith family spent two weeks in the Soviet Union. Samantha visited Moscow and Leningrad, met Valentina Tereshkova (the first woman in space), and stayed at the Artek children's camp on the Black Sea. At a press conference, she declared that Russian children are "just like us."

On her return to the United States, Samantha was named a "Goodwill Ambassador." She was interviewed many times on TV and, with the help of her father, wrote the book *Journey to the Soviet Union*. She also traveled to Japan to give a speech at the International Children's Symposium.

In 1984, Samantha hosted a presidential election special on TV. The following year, she got an acting part in a TV drama series called *Lime Street*. In August, thirteen-year-old Samantha and her father were returning home from filming when they were killed in a plane crash.

The Soviet Union issued a postage stamp in Samantha's honor, and a diamond and an asteroid were named after her. Maine erected a life-size statue of her, and her mother set up the Samantha Smith Foundation, dedicated to peace.

Samantha may not have changed the course of United States-Soviet relations, but her sunny smile and natural openness had a real impact on cultural relations. Ordinary Soviet people were fascinated by the sweet girl who seemed so unlike the warmongering Americans shown in political cartoons. And Americans had a rare glimpse of the Soviet Union: they saw that, after all, Soviet people were just ordinary people who wanted peace as much as they did.

BE FEARLESS, LIKE SAMANTHA SMITH!

Q *Two of your best friends aren't speaking to each other, and it's getting AWKWARD. They both expect you to take their side, and you feel torn. In fact, you just want to stay home and ignore both of them! What would Samantha Smith do?*

A Samantha Smith was raised to think of the Soviet Union as the enemy, and she was surprised to learn that Soviet people saw the United States in the same way! She'd probably remind you that there are usually two (or even three) sides to every story and advise you to listen carefully to both of your friends. Then perhaps you could organize a three-way peace conference in which you all get a chance to speak—and make up.

> God made the world for us to live together in peace and not fight.
>
> SAMANTHA SMITH

CARLOS ACOSTA

BALLET LEGEND

Growing up as a penniless street kid in a tough Havana neighborhood, Carlos Acosta seemed destined for a life of petty crime. Then his father managed to get him into ballet school, and Carlos danced his way out of poverty—and all the way to the top! A global superstar, he became the first black principal dancer at the Royal Ballet in London, England.

NAME: *Carlos Acosta*
BORN: June 2, 1973
NATIONALITY: Cuban
ROLE: Ballet dancer and director

Carlos Acosta was born in Havana to a black father and a white mother. He was the youngest of eleven children, and they all lived in a grimy, one-bedroom apartment with no running water. His family was so poor that his mother once served the children's pet rabbits for dinner.

As a child, Carlos ran wild with a gang of street kids. Around age nine, he began breakdancing and was so talented that crowds would gather to watch his moves. His father worried that Carlos's lifestyle would lead him into crime. When he heard that the ballet school provided free meals to its pupils, he sent his son for an audition. Carlos didn't know a thing about ballet, and he was NOT impressed—he wanted to be a soccer player, not a ballet dancer in tights!

Carlos got in, but he hated it. He kept skipping class to breakdance on street corners, so he was expelled. His father was furious and sent him to another ballet school. Here, Carlos finally started working—and discovered he was talented.

When he was sixteen, Carlos went to the Italian city of Turin on a year-long exchange program. While there, he scooped the gold medal in the Prix de Lausanne—an international competition. This was a life-changing moment for Carlos.

At the age of eighteen, Carlos became the English National Ballet's youngest principal dancer ever. A bad ankle injury forced him to take a break. Once recovered, Carlos toured with the National Ballet of Cuba and then danced with the Houston Ballet in Texas for five years.

In 1998, Carlos became the first black principal dancer at the Royal Ballet in London. He performed with them for seventeen years and was celebrated as the greatest male dancer of his generation. During this period, he penned his autobiography, *No Way Home*, as well as a magical novel about Cuba called *Pig's Foot*.

Carlos's own dance company, Acosta Danza, was set up in Cuba in 2015. He told reporters that to become a ballet star he'd had no choice but to leave Cuba. His dream is that things will be different for the Cuban stars of the future.

The Carlos Acosta International Dance Foundation supports young dancers from around the world. It was inspired by Carlos's own experience of being a poor kid who was given the chance to shine: he wanted to make that possible for other disadvantaged kids, too.

In 2019, it was announced that Carlos would become the new director of the Birmingham Royal Ballet in England. Carlos's rise from the slums of Havana to international ballet stardom is a pretty incredible rags-to-riches story!

BE FEARLESS, LIKE CARLOS ACOSTA!

Q *Ever since you were tiny, you've loved dancing. When you hear a tune, you just can't help moving along to it. You want to take dance classes, but your dad says it's a waste of money. He'd rather you focus on "boy stuff" like baseball or karate. What might Carlos Acosta do?*

A It was actually Carlos's dad who wanted him to take ballet. Carlos thought it was too girly, but he found it was the perfect way to express himself. He'd probably advise you to tell your dad that dancing feels like YOU. And if he won't give in, well then dance around wherever you are, whenever you can!

"DON'T REMAIN WHERE YOU ARE, BUT KEEP EVOLVING."

CARLOS ACOSTA

TAWAKKOL KARMAN

PEACEFUL PROTESTER

Despite being born into a male-dominated society in a country where criticizing your government was a big no-no, Tawakkol Karman wasn't prepared to keep her voice down. She saw political corruption and human rights abuses around her, and she wanted change. But she believed that the only way to fight against violence and repression was WITHOUT violence—and she became a pioneer for promoting peaceful protest in the Middle East.

NAME: *Tawakkol Karman*

BORN: February 7, 1979

NATIONALITY: Yemeni

ROLE: Human rights activist, journalist, and politician

Tawakkol Karman was born in the Arab country of Yemen. Her father was a lawyer and later a politician. He spoke out against government corruption, and Tawakkol was raised to care about suffering and injustice.

In 1990, North and South Yemen were unified. This led to civil war in 1994. When the North was triumphant, its repressive government took control of the whole country.

Fired up by political instability and the human rights abuses she witnessed, Tawakkol became a journalist. Her articles and films were often critical of the Yemeni government. In response, it placed restrictions on her and issued threats.

Did Tawakkol quieten down? Quite the opposite! She believed in freedom of speech. In 2005, she and several other women founded Woman Journalists Without Chains. They held weekly "sit-ins"—nonviolent demonstrations—in the capital, Sana'a. They demanded an end to corruption, freedom of expression, and civil rights, particularly for women.

Tawakkol told reporters that although she had every reason to be afraid for her safety, her desire for "dignity and freedom" meant that she would never allow that fear to get the better of her. Despite being abducted, imprisoned, and attacked, she built "a wall" between herself and the fear, keeping her eyes firmly on her dream.

When Tawakkol was first sent to prison, her husband spoke to the media about how proud he was of her. In Yemen, women who are perceived to have brought shame on their families are often criticized and even abandoned by them, so his actions were remarkable. Tawakkol was arrested many times, but instead of silencing her, the government was giving her a voice. More and more people heard about what she was trying to do and began to see her as a leader.

In early 2011, a revolutionary wave of protests, now known as the Arab Spring, swept through the Middle East and North Africa. The movement, in favor of democracy, demanded an end to oppression and corruption.

As governments across the Arab world began to topple, Tawakkol led a small protest against Yemen's president, Ali Abdullah Saleh, and was arrested. After her release, she didn't waste any time in organizing another demonstration. She spent nine months living in a tent, away from her husband and three children, leading peaceful protests and demanding the president's resignation. He was ousted in February 2012.

Tawakkol became known both as the "Mother of the Revolution" and the "Iron Woman." In 2011, she was awarded the Nobel Peace Prize in recognition of her peaceful struggle for democracy and women's rights. At the time, she was the joint youngest person ever to receive the award, as well as the first Yemeni, the first Arab woman, and the second Muslim woman to do so. That's quite a list!

> " I have always believed that resistance against repression and violence is possible without relying on similar repression and violence.

TAWAKKOL KARMAN

BE FEARLESS, LIKE TAWAKKOL KARMAN!

Q *You see a bunch of kids bullying a classmate. They throw some punches, trip him, and laugh cruelly when he hits the ground. You feel so mad that you're thinking of asking your friends to help you give the bullies a taste of their own medicine. What might Tawakkol Karman do?*

A Growing up, Tawakkol saw a lot of political violence, but she never for one second thought that more violence would solve anything. Perhaps she'd tell you that hurting someone back in a tit-for-tat way might feel satisfying at the time, but it could easily get out of hand and make things worse. Far better to tell a teacher, who can talk to the bullies and help your classmate.

DENG ADUT

REMARKABLE REFUGEE

When Deng Adut was just six years old, he was snatched from his mother's arms and forced to become a child soldier. For years, he witnessed violence, bloodshed, and death—horrors that no child should see. Miraculously, his brother helped him escape, and he became a refugee in Australia. Deng is a survivor —he turned his trauma into victory, teaching himself to read and eventually becoming a respected lawyer.

NAME: *Deng Adut*

BORN: circa 1983 (exact date unknown)
NATIONALITY: Sudanese-Australian
ROLE: Former child soldier, now a criminal lawyer

Deng Adut was born into a large family on the banks of the Nile River in what is now South Sudan. He and his seven brothers and sisters were raised on a banana farm.

In 1983, the year of Deng's birth, a vicious civil war broke out in Sudan. Deng was only six when the rebel army, which was fighting against the government, snatched him from his mother to make him a soldier. Along with many other children, Deng was forced to march barefoot to Ethiopia on a journey that took thirty-three days. Some died of thirst and starvation along the way.

Once in Ethiopia, the children were put through intense military training. Those who didn't obey orders were executed by a firing squad and their friends were forced to watch. Food was scarce, and Deng caught all kinds of nasty illnesses. Once he stepped on a nail, which led to an infection. The pain was almost unbearable, and his foot kept getting reinfected by a small insect called a "jigger" that buried deep into the wound. Deng says it nearly crippled him.

At the age of nine, Deng was taught how to use an AK-47 rifle. He says he was "expected to kill or be killed." At age twelve, he was shot in the back. While he was recovering, he met a soldier who, by chance, knew his older half-brother, John.

Ten years older than Deng, John had also been abducted from the family home as a youngster. He had thought Deng was dead. Determined to help his brother escape the war, John hid him under some corn sacks in a truck and, under cover of darkness, drove him over the border to Kenya. The two spent eighteen months in a refugee camp in Kenya before being granted a visa to travel to Australia as refugees.

Deng was now fourteen years old. Despite the horrors he had escaped, he found living in Australia very difficult. He didn't understand the culture, had hardly any education, and didn't speak English. By using dictionaries and watching *The Wiggles* TV show, Deng mastered the language. Living in a car, he did many odd jobs to survive. Meanwhile, he studied for the equivalent of a high school diploma, and in 2005 he won a scholarship to study law at Western Sydney University.

Deng and John both earned degrees in Australia. Deng went on to work as a criminal lawyer, and John returned to Sudan as an aid worker. It was there that he tragically lost his life in 2014 while helping civilians escape the conflict. As a tribute to his brother, Deng set up the John Mac Foundation, which provides higher-education scholarships for refugees in Australia and promotes justice in South Sudan.

In 2017, Deng released his best-selling memoir, *Songs of a War Boy*. That year he was named New South Wales Australian of the Year.

Deng returned to Sudan in 2012, where he was reunited with his mother. But he now considers Australia to be home. He says, *"My gratitude is to fellow Australians, for opening the door, not only to me but to all the other migrants like me."*

Q *You're feeling miserable. Your parents never stop criticizing you, school is awful, and your best friend just moved away. You can't see anything changing any time soon! What might Deng Adut do?*

A Deng Adut suffered unimaginable hardship in his young life, but somehow he found the strength to pick up the broken pieces and find a path to hope. We can't be sure what Deng would say, but he'd probably agree that yes, growing up can be tough. And then he'd remind you that you're unique and amazing! As he says, *"Try your best to be yourself and anything is possible."*

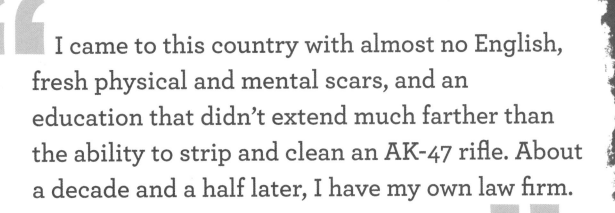

> I came to this country with almost no English, fresh physical and mental scars, and an education that didn't extend much farther than the ability to strip and clean an AK-47 rifle. About a decade and a half later, I have my own law firm.

DENG ADUT

39

JESSE MARTIN

LIONHEARTED SAILOR

Jesse Martin grew up on a diet of adventure, but even so, his dream to sail solo around the world seemed a little . . . unrealistic. He was only seventeen years old and far too inexperienced for such a treacherous journey! But on his 328-day voyage, Jesse showed people just how tough and determined he was, sailing into the record books as the youngest person ever to complete this incredible challenge.

NAME: *Jesse Martin*
BORN: August 26, 1981
NATIONALITY: German-Australian
ROLE: World record-breaking sailor

Jesse Martin had a more adventurous childhood than most. He was born in Germany while his parents were traveling in a camper van. It was clear that life was never going to be dull!

When Jesse was two, his family settled in Australia. Near a tropical rain forest in Queensland, his parents built a basic shack with no electricity or running water. Jesse and his younger brother, Beau, had complete freedom, enjoying everything the outdoors had to offer.

A few years later, Jesse's parents separated. His mother took her sons back to Melbourne, Australia. When Jesse was fourteen, his father bought a fourteen-foot (four-meter) catamaran and took his sons on a sailing trip—a mere 620 miles (1,000 km). The trio hadn't sailed before, but they were pretty good at it by the end of the two-month voyage!

The idea of sailing solo around the world fixed itself in Jesse's mind. When he was sixteen, he and Beau paddled kayaks along the coast of New Ireland in Papua New Guinea for five weeks. Soon after, Jesse connected with a yacht crew and sailed for three and a half months from Belize in Central America to the South Pacific.

Jesse didn't enjoy school and dreamed of adventure and independence. He was also inspired by David Dicks—an Australian who in 1996, at age eighteen, sailed around the world with assistance.

His parents, who had always encouraged Jesse and his brother to believe they could do ANYTHING, fully supported his dream. His mother even mortgaged her house to buy *Lionheart*, a thirty-four-foot (ten-meter) sailboat. On December 7, 1998, seventeen-year-old Jesse set sail from Melbourne on his 30,000-mile (50,000-km) around-the-world voyage.

Shortly after passing New Zealand, Jesse's boat tipped over—something that would happen again and again. Jesse could never sleep for more than twenty minutes at a time—he had to ensure he didn't hit a whale or an iceberg or another boat. He battled wild storms, monster waves, and extreme loneliness—he sighted dry land only three times during his voyage.

After 328 days at sea, Jesse returned to Australia, now eighteen years old. Twenty thousand people lined the streets to greet him. Incredibly, he had achieved what he set out to do.

Jesse filmed his voyage, and the footage became the basis of a documentary. His book *Lionheart: A Journey of the Human Spirit* has sold 110,000 copies worldwide. People were inspired by the story of how an ordinary schoolboy made his extraordinary (and a little bit crazy) dream come true.

BE FEARLESS, LIKE JESSE MARTIN!

Q *Lately you've felt like you haven't really achieved anything—well, nothing exceptional. You're average at school, average at sports, average at drawing, and even average-looking! Boring! What might Jesse Martin do?*

A Jesse Martin wasn't very good at schoolwork, but he did find his passion. He'd probably suggest that you think about what you really like doing and then go for it! We can't all set world records, but we can push our limits a little. Find what you're crazy about and take a step. You may surprise yourself.

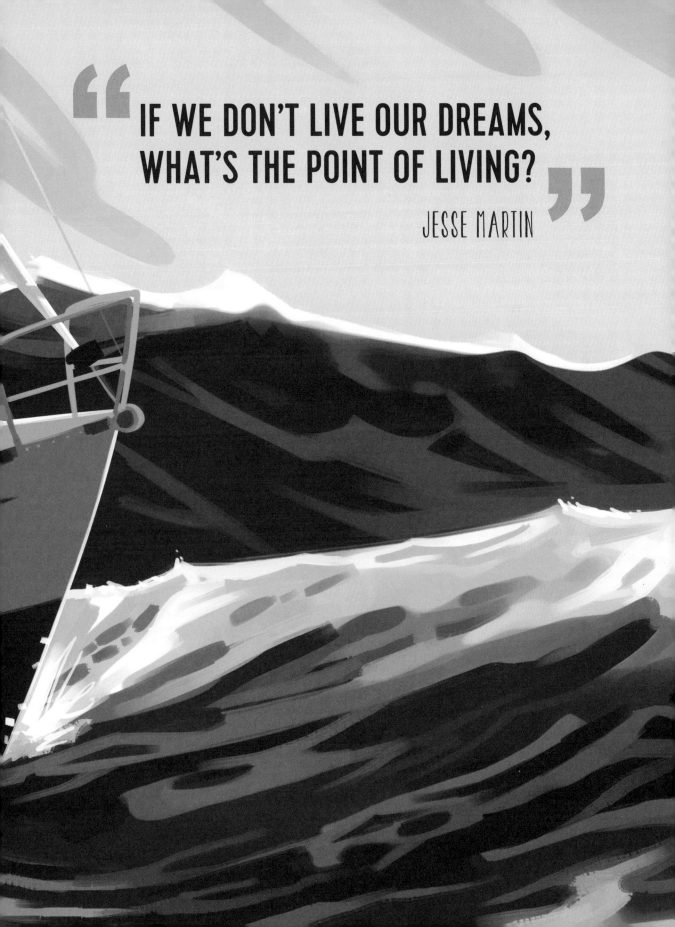

IQBAL MASIH

CHILDREN'S RIGHTS CHAMPION

Iqbal Masih was just four years old when he was forced into slavery. Despite years of terrible suffering, his spirit was never broken, and eventually he managed to escape. He became an activist, fighting to raise awareness of child labor. Iqbal knew he was risking his life by speaking up, but he was determined to help other child slaves. He paid the ultimate price when he was murdered at the age of twelve.

NAME: *Iqbal Masih*

BORN: 1983 (exact date unknown) **DIED:** April 16, 1995 (age twelve)

NATIONALITY: Pakistani

ROLE: Former child slave and children's rights activist

Iqbal was born in the city of Muridke, Pakistan. When he was a baby, his father abandoned the family, and his mother was left struggling to feed and clothe her children.

When Iqbal was four, his mother desperately needed a small amount of money, so she borrowed it from a carpet factory owner. In return, Iqbal was forced into "bonded labor," meaning he had to work for the factory owner as a carpet weaver until the debt had been paid off.

It's hard to imagine the suffering that Iqbal and the other child slaves in the factory endured. They had to weave for fourteen hours a day, six days a week, often chained to their looms. Because the windows were always kept closed to keep out insects, the heat was unbearable. The children were not allowed to speak to each other and received frequent beatings. If anyone tried to escape, they were threatened with being thrown into burning oil.

For the first year, Iqbal was paid nothing at all. After that, he was paid a tiny amount each day— but because he was often fined for mistakes and because interest was added to the loan, the debt was growing rather than shrinking. By the time Iqbal was ten years old, the family owed many times more than the original debt and there was little hope of it ever being paid off, however much he continued working.

Years of not having enough to eat and crouching over a loom all day meant that Iqbal was very short, with a hunched back. In fact, he was only half the height of an average ten-year-old. But there was something in his character that made him determined not to be broken. One day Iqbal happened to see a poster from the Bonded Labor Liberation Front (BLLF). It declared that bonded labor was illegal in Pakistan. Iqbal managed to make contact with BLLF activists, and they helped him escape from his life as a slave at the carpet factory.

Iqbal went on to attend the BLLF school in Lahore, Pakistan, and he got involved in demonstrations that protested against bonded child labor. He helped raise awareness of the issue, speaking to journalists about his own experiences and even addressing large crowds. In 1994, he was invited to the United States, where he was presented with the Youth in Action Award and visited schools and human rights groups. He was offered a full scholarship to study at Brandeis University in Massachusetts, and he spoke of becoming a lawyer.

Iqbal's activism made him many enemies in Pakistan, and he began to receive death threats. On Easter Sunday in 1995, he was cycling with two cousins on a lonely, dusty road when he was shot dead. No one has ever been held responsible for his murder, but many believe that he was killed by agents from the so-called "carpet mafia."

Five years after his death, Iqbal was awarded the World's Children's Prize for the Rights of the Child. It's incredible to think of what he achieved in his short, tragic life—just imagine what he might have gone on to do.

> ## "Children should have pens in their hands, not tools."
>
> ### IQBAL MASIH

BE FEARLESS, LIKE IQBAL MASIH!

Q *You're getting so fed up with school. You have to get up early, work like a slave all day—and then your parents and teachers get all worked up if you don't do your homework. It's just not fair, right? What would Iqbal Masih do?*

A Iqbal Masih knew what it was like to be a slave. It meant being chained to a loom all day. It meant being beaten for the slightest error. And it meant never going to school. Iqbal dreamed of being a lawyer, but he never had the chance. School might seem like a drag at times, but Iqbal would probably remind you to make the most of it—after all, having a good education gives you many more choices when you grow up.

GEORGE THE POET

URBAN WORDSMITH

George Mpanga was born in a tough part of London, England, in an area with few opportunities. In school, he began rapping about the injustice he saw around him. But George wanted to truly speak to his audience—and he discovered poetry. Boring? No way! This modern bard uses rhyme and rhythm to make you sit up and listen.

NAME: *George Mpanga*

BORN: January 14, 1991

NATIONALITY: British

ROLE: Spoken word artist

Born to Ugandan parents, George Mpanga was raised in a bad neighborhood in Harlesden, in northwest London. It's a place of poverty, where many young people turn to crime. His parents hoped for something better for George, and with their encouragement he managed to get into one of the country's best high schools.

George did well in school, but he started to feel that the outside world wasn't really interested in him or where he came from—a black boy from a poor neighborhood—and that made him mad. He turned to rap and grime (a form of dance music) as a way of expressing his frustration and began performing on street corners and in clubs at age fifteen.

George was admitted to Cambridge University to study politics, psychology, and sociology. While there, he saw that "spoken word poetry" rather than rap was a more direct way of speaking to his audience. And he had plenty to say! For George, poetry powerfully communicates the realities of life—things that need to be said. His YouTube videos attracted thousands of hits.

In 2012, during the Olympic Games in London, George posted "My City" on YouTube. The poem is about the sad, forgotten parts of London and opens with, *"My city has a lot of faces, some can be found in forgotten places . . . ."* His reputation started to grow, and he was commissioned to write the closer for the 2013 Monaco Formula One Grand Prix. He'd already written about the 2012 Formula One season: *"It's unpredictable as a flight of a kite, It's like the height of excitement, Like the fight of a titan . . . ."*

George released his first EP, *The Chicken and the Egg*, in 2014. His first poetry collection, *Search Party*, was published in 2015. He said, "We're all here looking for something, and my poems are my way of finding myself."

Performing as George the Poet, George has become a spokesperson for the issues faced by poor inner-city communities. He has performed in front of Queen Elizabeth in Westminster Abbey, at the opening ceremony of the Rugby World Cup, and before a huge global audience when he introduced the BBC live coverage of the wedding of Prince Harry and Meghan Markle.

In May 2019, George's podcast series *Have You Heard George's Podcast?* grabbed the main prize at the British Podcast awards. Blending poetry, journalism, storytelling, and music, it explores topics from inequality and racism to the tragic Grenfell Tower fire that killed seventy-two people in London in 2017.

Some have suggested that George should be a politician. But he believes he can achieve a lot more with his poetry. By rhyming his thoughts about race, class, injustice—and lots of other things—out loud, he wants to inspire people and to change minds.

BE FEARLESS, LIKE GEORGE THE POET!

Q *In school, your teachers don't seem to have a very high opinion of you. They're not mean or anything, but they seem to give the smart kids a lot more attention. You feel discouraged, like there's not much point in trying. What might George the Poet do?*

A Where George comes from, children aren't expected to amount to much. George defied just about all the odds to reach Cambridge University. He'd probably remind you that everyone has something they're good at, and he'd encourage you to believe in your own power. As he says in "1,2,1,2," there are *"seven billion people in the world but there's only one you!"*

> Some people use poetry to express heartache, but I use it to broadcast a message. My message is that everyone has something to contribute.
>
> GEORGE THE POET

THANDIWE CHAMA

AMAZING ACTIVIST

Thandiwe was born into terrible poverty, but she always knew that she wanted—and deserved—an education. When her community in Zambia was shattered by AIDS, her school was shut down. But eight-year-old Thandiwe turned her frustration into action, organizing a protest march. She went on to campaign for education for all and became a leader in raising awareness about HIV/AIDS.

NAME: *Thandiwe Chama*

BORN: February 15, 1991

NATIONALITY: Zambian

ROLE: Education activist
for those living with HIV/AIDS

When Thandiwe Chama was just eight, her school closed because there weren't enough teachers. The tragic reason for this was that many of them had died of AIDS—a disease that was tearing through her homeland of Zambia.

Thandiwe wanted to go to school. She had been born into poverty, and she saw that an education could lead her out of hardship and toward something better. She persuaded many of her schoolmates to join her on a protest march. It paid off, because they became students at a neighboring school.

Fired up by her success, Thandiwe began to campaign for a better education for all Zambian children. Her amazing efforts brought about many changes. In 2007, the sixteen-year-old's grit and determination were recognized with the International Children's Peace Prize Award.

Thandiwe put her prize money to good use. The school she had attended had no roof or windows, so she fixed that. Then she arranged for new classrooms and a library to be built, as well as a science laboratory.

The HIV/AIDS epidemic was devastating Zambia and threatening its development. One reason for this was that the people with important roles, such as teachers and farmers, were dying.

Thandiwe saw that the key to addressing the problem was educating people about the disease. She became convinced that all children should understand how AIDS is spread, so she wrote a book called *The Chicken with AIDS* to be used as an educational tool in schools.

Thandiwe also believed in the power of making small changes, starting in her own community. She spoke to other people about AIDS whenever she had the chance, encouraging them to speak openly about the subject. She was also behind a program in which people took fruit to children who were sick in the nearby hospital. She helped people to get tested for the HIV virus—even accompanying them herself if need be.

Continuing to fight for children in Zambia and around the world, Thandiwe has given speeches at many international conferences. She speaks of her belief that EVERY child in the world has a voice—regardless of whether they're rich or poor, black or white, male or female—and that their voice deserves to be heard.

Thandiwe has said that one of the most important things for her was learning that children have rights: *"At school I learned about rights. And I knew then that this was something I wanted to fight for."*

BE FEARLESS, LIKE THANDIWE CHAMA!

Q *Funding problems mean that your local public library may have to close down. You feel really worried because you love reading and you use the library a lot. But you also feel powerless. What might Thandiwe Chama do?*

A When Thandiwe's school closed, she must have wondered what on earth an eight-year-old could do about it. Quite a bit, it turns out! We can't know for sure what she'd advise, but she'd probably suggest talking to your teachers and classmates. Perhaps you could organize a mini protest? Or you could write a joint letter to your Congressperson or state legislator? Little things can lead to bigger things— and you'll probably feel a lot better for trying.

" When you educate a child, you educate the nation. And an educated society is a developed society.

THANDIWE CHAMA "

RYAN HRELJAC

FANTASTIC FUNDRAISER

Most of us take clean drinking water for granted—turn on a faucet and there it is! When six-year-old Ryan Hreljac discovered this wasn't the case for everyone, it really bothered him. People were dying for lack of clean water, and he wanted to do something about it. Ryan started by saving up to pay for a new well in Africa—and he ended up founding a charity that has improved the lives of thousands.

NAME: *Ryan Hreljac*

BORN: May 31, 1991

NATIONALITY: Canadian

ROLE: Clean-water activist and founder of Ryan's Well Foundation

When Ryan Hreljac was six years old, he made a shocking discovery. His teacher explained how countless children in Africa had to walk miles each day just to fetch water—and even then it was often not clean. As a result of drinking dirty water, millions of people were getting ill and dying of deadly illnesses like typhoid.

Ryan had never really thought about it before, but he realized how unfair it was that he could have a drink of clean water whenever he wanted one, but others couldn't. And he decided to do something about it. He went home and pleaded with his parents to help. They told Ryan that if he was prepared to do chores around the house, they would give him extra allowance to save up.

Ryan started by vacuuming the house—and in four months he had saved $53. He hoped it would be enough to build a new well in an African country like Uganda. But after looking into it, he learned that the cost of a well would be closer to $1,500.

Ryan was pretty determined, though—he was going to raise that money! He started talking to anyone and everyone about his fundraising efforts and encouraged them to get involved, too. Within a year, $2,270 had been raised and the media picked up the story. In January 1999, a well was drilled in a Ugandan village next to a school called Angolo Primary. Ryan's school in Canada began to communicate with Angolo Primary, and in 2000 Ryan flew out to Uganda.

Five thousand children lined the roads, waiting to meet him. During his visit, Ryan bonded with a boy named Jimmy Akana. He told Ryan that before the well was dug, he used to get up at midnight and walk three miles (five kilometers) to a swamp to fetch water, and then walk three miles back. And what's more, he had to make this journey three times every day to get enough water for everyone in his family.

Jimmy was later caught up in the crossfire of Uganda's civil war. His parents disappeared and he was captured and trained as a child soldier. He managed to escape, and in 2003 Ryan's family successfully adopted him. Incredibly, he was now Ryan's brother!

Ryan's Well Foundation was founded in 2001. Its mission is to provide access to clean water in the world's poorest regions, as well as educating communities about the importance of hygiene and clean water. The charity has now developed more than 1,400 clean-water projects, improving the lives of almost a million people.

Meanwhile, Ryan continues to spread his message around the world. He has met famous people like Pope John Paul II and conservationist Dr. Jane Goodall. He has appeared on TV and won many awards for his incredible fundraising efforts. Countless young people have been motivated by his public speaking. As Ryan says, *"Everyone has the ability to make a profound impact on the lives of others . . . . Whether the cause is water or something else, just be naïve enough to think like a first grader."*

BE FEARLESS, LIKE RYAN HRELJAC!

Q *You see a TV show about critically endangered Bornean orangutans and it really gets to you. You decide to do a sponsored run to raise funds, but your parents encourage you to choose a different cause—why not something closer to home like helping homeless people or supporting cancer research? What might Ryan Hreljac do?*

A This is the deal: there are a lot of problems in the world. True, some might be more urgent than others, but they all need action. We can't be sure what Ryan Hreljac would tell you, but he'd probably say that if you feel passionately about something, then you're more likely to be successful in your fundraising efforts. The orangutans need people to help them, too—so go for it!

> I always thought the world is like a great big puzzle and we all have to figure out where our pieces fit. For me, it's water.

RYAN HRELJAC

BOYAN SLAT

INSPIRING INVENTOR

When Boyan Slat discovered just how much plastic was clogging up the world's oceans, his first thought was, *"Why don't we clean it up?"* Despite being told over and over again that it couldn't be done, he preferred to focus on COULD—and he got to work inventing a solution. Fast-forward several years, and Boyan's Ocean Cleanup project is the largest cleanup in history.

NAME: **Boyan Slat**

BORN: July 27, 1994

NATIONALITY: Dutch

ROLE: Inventor and founder of the Ocean Cleanup

• •

Boyan Slat's talent for invention was obvious from an early age. He built tree houses and zip lines and liked to make explosions! When he was fourteen, he set a Guinness World Record by launching 213 water rockets at the same time from his hometown of Delft in the Netherlands.

In the summer of 2011, sixteen-year-old Boyan visited Greece with his family. While scuba diving, he noticed that the sea's beauty was spoiled by something—PLASTIC. Boyan was shocked that there seemed to be more plastic bags than fish in the sea. He promised himself that he would find a solution.

Researching online, Boyan discovered how enormous the problem is. Because plastic is useful to humans and because it is so cheap, it is everywhere. As a result, eight million tons of plastic end up in the oceans each year, where it causes terrible harm to marine life.

Boyan was repeatedly told the plastic problem was so huge there was no point in even trying to fix it, but he didn't believe that argument! As he says, *"History is basically a list of things that couldn't be done and then were done."*

For a school project, Boyan presented an idea for a long sea barrier that would catch passing pieces of plastic. Two years later, while studying for a degree in aerospace engineering, he was invited to do a TEDx talk about his proposed solution. He jumped at the chance, and within a week, a video of the talk had gone viral. Boyan sought the advice of as many inventors and businesspeople as possible to help develop his idea. Then a few months later, he dropped out of college and set up a nonprofit company called the Ocean Cleanup.

Boyan's project has attracted millions of dollars in donations, allowing System 001, or "Wilson," to be built. These long floating tubes are designed to trap ocean plastic without harming marine life. The first tube was launched off the coast of San Francisco at the end of 2018. It did collect plastic, but unfortunately it then released it back into the sea. The equipment was also damaged by wind and waves.

After months of repair work, a second attempt with the tube began in June 2019. We don't know whether it will ultimately prove successful, but we get the sense that as long as plastic continues to clog up the oceans, Boyan won't stop working on a solution. He doesn't think in terms of failure, but sees problems as opportunities to learn from —as bumps on the road to success. As he says, *"I'm an obsessive and I like it!"*

• •

> " Pessimism is what preserves the status quo, and optimism is what brings us forward. "
>
> BOYAN SLAT

BE FEARLESS, LIKE BOYAN SLAT!

Q *Your teacher has given you a difficult science project to complete. Over the weekend, you spend hours working on a solution to the problem and you think you've found it! And then you realize the problem is still as big as ever. You just want to give up! What might Boyan Slat do?*

A Boyan Slat is no stranger to disappointment—he's had to watch his Ocean Cleanup plan suffer real setbacks. Chances are he'd tell you that sometimes things don't work out just as you want them to, but if you can learn anything from your efforts, then your time hasn't been wasted. So take a break, gather your thoughts, and get right back to work!

VICTORIA ARLEN

PHENOMENAL PARALYMPIAN

At the age of eleven, Victoria Arlen slipped into a deep coma. When she came around age thirteen, she couldn't see, move, or talk—and had no way of telling anyone she was awake! Victoria spent another two years in this state, passing the time by making plans: she WOULD get better and she'd give back to the world. Not only did Victoria recover, she became a swimming gold medalist at the Paralympics and defied doctors by walking again.

NAME: *Victoria Arlen*

BORN: September 26, 1994

NATIONALITY: American

ROLE: Paralympian swimmer and TV personality

• •

Victoria Arlen was the first baby of triplets to arrive. She and her brothers had an ordinary, happy childhood. Then, when she was eleven years old, everything changed.

Victoria had always been healthy and active, but she began to feel tired and sick. She lost a lot of weight and had horrible pains. Soon she lost movement in her legs and arms, and then she couldn't swallow or speak properly. It must have been terrifying, especially since doctors weren't sure what was wrong with her.

Everything went dark for Victoria and she has no memory of the next two years. In fact, she had slipped into a coma—a state where a person is alive but has no awareness of their surroundings. It's kind of like being asleep, but you can't be woken up.

In 2009, Victoria came out of her coma, but she was "locked in." This means her mind had woken up, but her body hadn't—she could hear conversations around her, but she couldn't move, see, or communicate with anyone. By this time, doctors had diagnosed a rare condition. She even heard them telling her parents that she would probably die.

But Victoria wasn't ready to die, and her family wasn't ready to lose hope. They continued to speak to her, giving her the will to fight. She says she made a promise to God: *"If you give me a second chance, I will use my voice to change the world."*

Victoria was having up to twenty seizures a day, so doctors gave her a sleeping drug to calm her body. Soon after, she "locked eyes" with her mother, who sensed that something had changed.

She asked her daughter to blink if she could hear her—and miraculously, Victoria blinked.

Then the long road to recovery started. Victoria had to relearn the simplest of tasks, like wiggling her fingers. Then she had to learn how to eat and speak again. After missing five years of school, she returned to classes in 2010.

Paralyzed from the waist down, Victoria was told she would never walk again. She was determined to be active though, and learned to swim without the use of her legs. At the age of seventeen, she was part of the United States swim team competing at the 2012 Paralympics in London. She won three silver medals, plus the gold medal for the one-hundred meters freestyle—for which she set a world record.

Thrust into the media spotlight, Victoria began traveling around the world and inspiring audiences at speaking events. In 2015, her ability in front of the camera landed her a job as a reporter for the sports channel ESPN.

Victoria had never really accepted that she wouldn't walk again, and she began intensive daily therapy. Doctors were doubtful, but in late 2015 Victoria took her first small steps. Five months later, she was walking with leg braces, but no crutches. Later, despite having no feeling in her legs, she started running and even competed on the TV show *Dancing with the Stars*.

Victoria's recovery has defied all the odds. She, puts her success down to her family, her faith, and her motto: *"Face It, Embrace It, Defy It, Conquer It!"*

• •

BE FEARLESS, LIKE VICTORIA ARLEN!

Q *You told a teacher that you want to be an actor one day, and he actually smirked! You know you're shy and your voice often comes out as a squeak in class, but deep down you know you were born for the stage. Or were you?*

A Victoria Arlen had to put up with a lot of people telling her what she couldn't do: she'd never recover, she'd never talk, she'd never walk. She decided early on that she'd only accept those verdicts once she'd thrown everything she had at her challenges—SHE was in charge. So she'd probably tell you to smirk right back at your teacher (maybe not in his face), start acting, and show people what you can do!

> " I learned early on that extraordinary challenges lead to extraordinary victories. "
>
> VICTORIA ARLEN

ALEXANDRA SCOTT

FABULOUS FUNDRAISER

Ever heard of the expression, *"When life gives you lemons . . . make lemonade"*? Well, that's exactly what brave four-year-old Alex did. Despite being very sick with cancer, Alex told her parents she wanted to set up a lemonade stand so she could help other kids suffering from the illness. Today, Alex's foundation has raised millions of dollars to fund cutting-edge research into childhood cancer.

NAME: *Alexandra Scott*

BORN: **January 18, 1996** DIED: **August 1, 2004** (age eight)

NATIONALITY: **American**

ROLE: **Fundraiser for research into childhood cancer**

Just before Alex's first birthday, her parents realized something wasn't quite right. They thought she had some kind of stomach problem, but hospital tests showed she had a huge tumor growing on her spine. Doctors broke the devastating news that Alex had neuroblastoma—a type of childhood cancer.

Alex's parents were told that if she survived, she would probably never learn to walk. Just two weeks later, Alex moved her leg when her parents asked her to kick. This may seem like a little thing, but they realized Alex was a fighter!

Alex's parents were right: their daughter was fiercely determined and spirited. By the age of two, she was crawling and standing with the aid of leg braces. Then she astounded doctors by learning to walk.

The day after Alex's fourth birthday, her parents learned that her cancer had started to grow again. She would need a stem cell transplant. Alex told her parents that when she came out of the hospital, she wanted to set up a lemonade stand. She said the money raised could be given to doctors to help other kids with cancer, because *"all kids deserve to have their tumors go away."*

Later that year, Alex set up a lemonade stand in her front yard with the help of her older brother, Patrick. It raised an incredible $2,000 for her hospital. As Alex continued to fight her illness, she also continued setting up yearly lemonade stands in her front yard. News of her amazing fundraising efforts spread, and people from all around the world began to hold their own lemonade events, too. The money they raised was also donated to research into childhood cancers.

In 2004, Alex appeared on *The Oprah Winfrey Show* and told the audience how she made her lemonade. Two months later, she died at home. During her short life, she helped raise more than $1 million to help find a cure for the disease she was fighting.

In 2005, Alex's parents set up Alex's Lemonade Stand Foundation (ALSF) to continue the fundraising that Alex began. With more than $150 million raised so far, it's now one of the biggest contributors to research into childhood cancers. The funds are also used to help support the families of children living with cancer.

On the anniversary of Alex's death in 2017, her brother Patrick posted a moving letter to his sister online. He wrote, *"More than anything, I remember you for what you taught me .... You, as a terminally ill child, were still appreciative of the blessings that you had .... Though you were never old in age, you were old in wisdom."*

BE FEARLESS, LIKE ALEXANDRA SCOTT!

Q *You're really looking forward to summer, and then OUCH! While playing soccer with your friends, you end up with a broken leg. Summer ruined, right? What would Alexandra Scott do?*

A Alex knew all too well that sometimes life throws sour lemons at us. But she found her own way of turning that sourness into sweet lemonade. We don't know exactly what she'd advise, but she'd probably sympathize with you—breaking a leg *is* bad luck—and then she'd remind you to think about all the things you can still do. We can't change the things that happen to us, but we can decide how to respond to them.

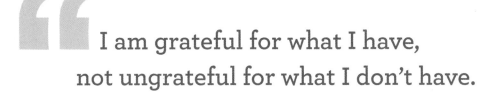

" I am grateful for what I have,
not ungrateful for what I don't have. "

ALEXANDRA SCOTT

SONITA ALIZADEH

REBELLIOUS RAPPER

When sixteen-year-old Sonita learned that her mother was planning to sell her into marriage, she wasn't about to go along with it. Instead, she wrote the powerful rap song "Daughters for Sale" and posted a music video on YouTube. It quickly went viral, and she was offered a scholarship to study in the United States. Sonita was safe, but she didn't stop there. She continues to fight —and rap—for an end to child marriage.

Sonita Alizadeh

BORN: **1996** (exact date unknown)
NATIONALITY: **Afghan**
ROLE: **Activist and rapper fighting to end child marriage**

Sonita Alizadeh was six years old when her family fled to Iran from Afghanistan to escape the extremist Taliban regime. As a refugee with no identity papers—Sonita is not even sure of her birth date—she had no right to an education. Instead, she was forced to work as a child laborer and often didn't have enough to eat.

Sonita's father died when she was ten, and her mother struggled to support the family. That's when Sonita learnt that her mother was planning to sell her into marriage, which was the tradition for young Afghan girls. Sonita's mother had been a child bride herself at the age of thirteen. Luckily, Sonita's marriage arrangement fell through. Sonita had seen many of her friends forced into marriage, and she understood the pain that it could bring.

As a way of expressing her feelings, Sonita started writing pop songs such as "Child Labor," but she found pop music too slow. As she says, _"It couldn't hold the story I wanted to share with the world."_ After hearing the music of the American rapper Eminem, she realized that rap had the power to share her message. She couldn't even understand Eminem's lyrics, but she loved the sense of urgency that she found in his delivery.

Because it's against the law in Iran for women to sing or rap in public, Sonita had to be incredibly careful about who saw her lyrics. Although it was risky, she began making secret recordings of her songs—and she even won $1,000 after entering an American competition to make a music video.

By the age of sixteen, Sonita was living alone in Iran's capital, Tehran, because her family had returned to Afghanistan. Her brother was to be married, and her mother needed money in order to buy his bride. That's when Sonita discovered that once again her family was planning to sell her into marriage—in exchange for $9,000.

Sonita wasn't about to let go of her dreams ,though! She decided to rebel in the only way she knew how, writing "Daughters for Sale." An Iranian filmmaker helped her make a music video that was posted on YouTube. In it, Sonia can be seen in a wedding dress, rapping her powerful message, _"I scream to make up for a woman's lifetime of silence . . . I scream for the body exhausted in its cage—a body that broke under the price tags you put on it."_

The video quickly went viral, inspiring many Afghan women and winning admiration around the world. Sonita hadn't expected this—the video had been directed at her family. But when she was offered a scholarship to a high school in the United States, she grabbed the chance.

Since moving to the United States, Sonita has continued to fight for an end to child marriage, rapping her message to enthralled audiences, meeting world leaders, and sharing a stage with influential activists. Each year, there are 12,000 child brides around the world—and that's something Sonita is determined to change.

BE FEARLESS, LIKE SONITA ALIZADEH!

Q *Your parents have decided you're going to be a doctor. You're great at science, good at math. The only problem is you don't want that at all! You've always been good at drama, and that's what makes you feel happy. What might Sonita Alizadeh do?*

A It's really no fun feeling pressured to do something that doesn't feel right for you. Sonita understood her mother was only following tradition and wanted the best for her—it was up to Sonita to convince her otherwise. She'd probably tell you to respectfully speak to your parents about your dreams—and to *show* them how happy drama makes you. But even if you can't convince them, you need to remember it's your life. Try to do what makes you happy.

> "When my mother told me they would have to sell me, I couldn't breathe. I couldn't speak."

SONITA ALIZADEH

MALALA YOUSAFZAI

COURAGEOUS ACTIVIST

Malala Yousafzai has a passion for learning, but when she was eleven years old, the hard-line Taliban movement banned girls from going to school. Malala wasn't about to give up her right to an education without a fight—and she answered violence with words. When Malala was fifteen, a Taliban gunman shot her in the head. But even though she almost died, her voice has only grown louder . . .

NAME: *Malala Yousafzai*

BORN: July 12, 1997

NATIONALITY: Pakistani

ROLE: Activist for girls' education

In Malala's homeland of Pakistan, many children don't have the chance to go to school, but the situation is even worse for girls. More than twenty percent of girls are forced into marriage while they are still children.

Malala was lucky to be born into a family that considered education to be important for both boys and girls. Her father had been bullied in school, and this gave him a hatred of injustice. His five sisters received no education at all, and he thought that was plain wrong—so he decided to set up a girls' school. Malala was one of its students.

For Malala, everything changed when the Taliban—an extremist Islamic movement—took control of the Swat Valley where she lived. As well as banning things like watching television and dancing, the Taliban stopped girls from going to school.

Malala wasn't prepared to accept this—she wanted an education! In fact, she believed it was her RIGHT. She began to blog anonymously under the name of Gul Makai for the BBC Urdu language site. In *The Diary of a Pakistani Schoolgirl*, Malala described her fears, her desire to go to school, and the horrors of Taliban rule. When her identity was revealed, Malala bravely began to speak out in public. In 2011, she was nominated for an International Children's Peace Prize and was awarded Pakistan's National Youth Peace Prize.

By now, the Taliban's grip on the region was lessening and girls were allowed back to elementary school. Malala continued to speak out though, and she began to receive death threats. In October 2012, she was on her way home from school when a masked Taliban gunman boarded her bus and shot her in the head. Critically injured and close to death, Malala was flown to Birmingham, England, for treatment. Her shattered skull was repaired, and she was given a hearing device to replace her destroyed eardrum.

Malala was eventually well enough to start attending school in Birmingham. Meanwhile, her story had made headlines around the world. In Pakistan, an education fund was launched in her honor, and also the Malala Fund was set up to support education for girls across the globe.

On July 12, 2013, on her sixteenth birthday—now called Malala Day—Malala gave a speech at the United Nations in New York. Later that year, her bestselling memoir, *I Am Malala*, was published. In 2014, she became the youngest person ever to receive the Nobel Peace Prize.

In 2017, Malala began studying for a degree at Oxford University, England. But this certainly hasn't stopped her from continuing to speak up for the 130 million girls around the world who have no chance of going to school. Her 2019 book, *We Are Displaced*, tells the stories of refugee girls pushed out of their countries by violence. Speaking of the girls' courage, Malala says: *"Either you lose hope completely and you shatter and break into pieces, or you become so resilient that no one can break you anymore."*

BE FEARLESS, LIKE MALALA YOUSAFZAI!

Q *You love designing things, and you dream of being an engineer. Your dad thinks that's a strange job for a woman though, and he's encouraging you to choose another path. What might Malala do?*

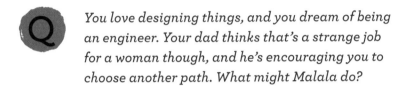

A In Pakistan, many girls don't go to school at all. Malala thought this was very wrong, and when the Taliban tried to ban girls from learning, she certainly wasn't going to be quiet about it! We can't be sure what Malala would advise you, but she'd probably tell you to speak calmly to your dad about the *many* reasons why you would make an excellent engineer. Oh, and she'd probably tell you to dream big and hold on to that dream.

" The hardest thing is to see a girl nearly my age, with all the dreams and aspirations that I have, stuck in a situation she didn't create and unable to choose her own future. "

MALALA YOUSAFZAI

ANN MAKOSINSKI

TRAILBLAZING INVENTOR

As a child, Ann Makosinski was encouraged to make her own toys—and that's what brought out her amazing talent for invention. She was just fifteen when she created the battery-free Hollow Flashlight—a flashlight powered completely by the heat of a human hand. Ann speaks to audiences around the world and has made it her mission to inspire others: dream big, don't waste your time, and you *can* change the world!

Ann Makosinski

BORN: October 3, 1997

NATIONALITY: Canadian

ROLE: Tech inventor

When Ann Makosinski was growing up in Victoria, British Columbia—a province in Canada—her parents didn't buy her expensive toys or let her watch much TV. And she wasn't allowed to play video games or have a cell phone.

Did this hold Ann back? Definitely not! Her parents encouraged her to enjoy the natural world around her and to use her imagination. One of her first toys was a box of transistors. She would spend hours taking apart electronics components or creating gizmos from bits and pieces lying around the house.

From the age of seven, Ann invented things for local science fairs. When she reached high school, she admits she was a "science weirdo" and a nerd compared to the popular kids, but she soon saw that this didn't matter one bit.

Ann had a friend in the Philippines—where her mother comes from—who was doing badly at school because she had no light to do her homework by at night. This really bothered Ann, so at the age of fifteen she set out to find a solution. She realized that humans produce "wasted" heat and that this thermal energy could surely be put to good use. It took Ann about six months to create her prototype of the Hollow Flashlight—a battery-free flashlight powered only by the warmth of a human hand.

The Hollow Flashlight invention won in Ann's age category at the Google Science Fair and made her a teen superstar. In 2013, she was included in *Time* magazine's "Thirty under thirty" feature, and she was invited to appear on shows such as *The Tonight Show Starring Jimmy Fallon*.

It was on the *Tonight Show* that Ann presented her next big invention to Jimmy Fallon and the public: the eDrink. This is a mug that uses the heat from a hot drink as it cools down and converts it into an electric current. This can then be used to charge a cell phone and power it for up to thirty minutes.

Since her rise to fame, Ann has taken part in five TEDx talks—online speaking events in which thinkers and scientists come together to present their ideas. In 2017, she was listed in *Forbes* magazine's "Thirty under thirty" list—a huge achievement. Oh, and she's also had a meteorite named after her!

One of Ann's most-watched TEDx talks has the title, "Why I Don't Use a Smartphone." This is a message that Ann is passionate about. Smartphones have their uses, of course, but they also stop people from getting on with things and actually doing stuff. Her advice is, *"Next time you pick up your phone, think of all the possibilities off your phone and not on it."*

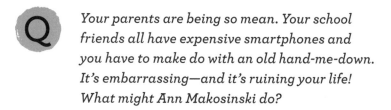

BE FEARLESS, LIKE ANN MAKOSINSKI!

Q *Your parents are being so mean. Your school friends all have expensive smartphones and you have to make do with an old hand-me-down. It's embarrassing—and it's ruining your life! What might Ann Makosinski do?*

A When Ann was growing up, her parents didn't buy her the latest gadgets. In fact, they told her to make her own! They weren't being mean, though. They realized that this would help develop her creativity. We can't be sure what Ann's advice would be, but she'd likely tell you that having the latest smartphone isn't really going to change your life. On the other hand, taking time to develop new interests might just lead to exciting adventures!

> " Not being given everything encourages you to create . . . . That was one of the first steps for me learning to invent things. "
>
> ANN MAKOSINSKI

FELIX FINKBEINER

AWESOME ENVIRONMENTALIST

Felix Finkbeiner was just nine years old when he had an amazing idea. If a million trees could be planted in every country, then perhaps the world's dwindling forests could be restored? The result was a global kids' movement—Plant-for-the-Planet. And ten years later, fourteen billion trees have been planted. Felix hasn't stopped there, though—he now has his eyes set on one trillion trees.

NAME: **_Felix Finkbeiner_**

BORN: October 8, 1997

NATIONALITY: German

ROLE: Environmentalist and founder of Plant-for-the-Planet

When he was nine, Felix was asked to prepare a presentation on climate change for a school project. While researching the topic online, he stumbled across the story of Wangari Maathai. Little did Felix know that this would be the start of something BIG!

Wangari Maathai was from Kenya. After studying biological sciences in the United States, she returned home and saw that the destruction of forests was having a terrible impact on Kenya's environment. Her solution? She encouraged communities to plant trees— thirty million of them in thirty years! She won the Nobel Peace Prize in 2004 because peace depends on a secure, safe environment on Earth.

Felix felt inspired by her story. He told his classmates that trees "capture" carbon dioxide and release oxygen, and he reasoned that planting millions of them could be the answer to the world's human-made carbon emissions problem. He ended his presentation with the words: _"Let's plant a million trees in every country in the world!"_ Felix's teacher was impressed and asked him to repeat the presentation for the school's principal and the other classes.

Two weeks later, Felix planted his first tree—a crab apple—at his school. A local journalist reported the story, and word soon spread. Before long, schoolchildren all across Germany were planting trees. As more and more were planted, a website was launched to track the numbers. In just one year, it recorded that 50,000 seedlings were planted.

Felix named his campaign Plant-for-the-Planet. When he was ten years old, he gave a speech to the European Parliament. Then, when he was thirteen, he was invited to speak to the United Nations General Assembly in New York. Felix told his audience, _"If you let a monkey choose if he wants one banana now or six bananas later, the monkey will always choose the one banana now . . . . We children understood we cannot trust that adults alone will save our future. To do that, we have to take our future in our hands."_

With the help of the United Nations, Plant-for-the-Planet "academies" have been set up around the world. At free events, children become "climate justice ambassadors" and learn how to organize tree-planting in their own communities. More than fourteen billion trees in 130 countries have now been planted.

In 2017, Felix launched Trillion Trees. The plan is now to get a million children to become climate justice ambassadors and plant a trillion trees (that's 1,000 billion, by the way!)—150 for each person on Earth.

BE FEARLESS, LIKE FELIX FINKBEINER!

Q *Your parents know all about global warming. They've heard the news, they've seen the TV programs, and you've even heard them talking to their friends about how sad it all is. So WHY aren't they doing anything about it?*

A Felix knows that action is the key to solving the climate crisis. We can't be sure what he'd suggest, but he might advise you to lead by example—make plenty of changes in your own lifestyle and your parents may just follow suit! As one of Felix's famous slogans goes, *"Stop talking and start planting!"*

> We children know adults know the challenges and they know the solutions . . . . We don't know why there is so little action.

FELIX FINKBEINER

SHEKU KANNEH-MASON

SUPERSTAR CELLIST

Born into a musical family, Sheku Kanneh-Mason grew up surrounded by the sounds of his siblings practicing their instruments. In 2016, he became the first black person ever to win the BBC Young Musician of the Year award, and his star has continued to rise. You know you're getting famous when Meghan Markle gives you a call, right? That's how Sheku ended up performing at the royal wedding in 2018—and became a global star.

NAME: *Sheku Kanneh-Mason*
BORN: April 4, 1999
NATIONALITY: British
ROLE: Cellist

Sheku Kanneh-Mason grew up in the English city of Nottingham. His parents aren't musicians, but there's definitely a musical gene in the family—all seven children play an instrument to a high standard! The oldest, Isata, was incredibly talented at the piano and was accepted to the Junior Academy of the Royal Academy of Music in London when she was just eight.

Sheku began violin lessons when he was six, but he says he wanted to "outdo" his brother, Braimah, and play a larger instrument—so he switched to the cello. He immediately impressed his teachers with his talent and ability to play from memory. His parents have spoken of how they were often woken up at 5:00 a.m. by Sheku and Braimah practicing!

At the age of nine, Sheku passed a high-level cello exam with flying colors. He went on to win a scholarship to the Royal Academy of Music.

In 2015, six of the seven siblings took part in the TV show *Britain's Got Talent*. They reached the semifinal and judge David Walliams told them they had made classical music popular again. The following year, seventeen-year-old Sheku really caught the eye of the world when he won the BBC Young Musician of the Year award. In the final, he performed Shostakovich's Cello Concerto No. 1 on a 400-year-old cello. His performance was described as "electric."

Sheku was the first black person ever to win the award, which was hugely significant. Classical music is a cultural area where black people are underrepresented. Sheku and several of his siblings play in the Chineke! Orchestra—the first orchestra in Europe made up of young black and minority ethnic musicians.

By now, Sheku was in great demand as a performer, but he was also studying for exams in music, math, and physics in school. At the end of 2016, he signed a recording deal with Decca Classics. His first album, *Inspiration*, went to number one on the UK classical album chart. It features a selection of music, from Shostakovich's Cello Concerto No. 1 to Bob Marley's "No Woman, No Cry." It went viral and clocked more than one million streams on Spotify in its first month.

When Sheku performed at Prince Harry and Meghan Markle's wedding in May 2018, two billion people watched around the world—enough to make the most experienced performer a little anxious. But Sheku says he wasn't nervous—and it was the first wedding he'd ever been to!

Sheku doesn't seem fazed by his fame, still finding time to play soccer and hang out with friends. As he says, *"I'm very lucky . . . I've always been able to balance music with life."*

BE FEARLESS, LIKE SHEKU KANNEH-MASON!

Q *You've been having piano lessons for a few years now, but your heart isn't really in it. Really you want to play the guitar. You don't want to tell your parents, though—all that money wasted on the wrong instrument! What might Sheku Kanneh-Mason do?*

A Sheku started with the violin, but he knew it wasn't his thing. He'd probably suggest asking your parents if you can at least try a guitar lesson. Whatever happens, the piano lessons won't be a waste of time. Researchers have shown that learning an instrument makes you smarter and more creative!

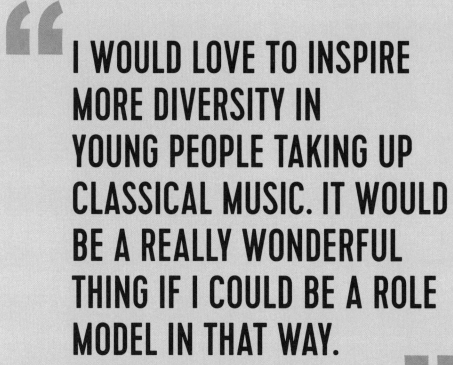

"I WOULD LOVE TO INSPIRE MORE DIVERSITY IN YOUNG PEOPLE TAKING UP CLASSICAL MUSIC. IT WOULD BE A REALLY WONDERFUL THING IF I COULD BE A ROLE MODEL IN THAT WAY."

SHEKU KANNEH-MASON

EMMA GONZÁLEZ

STUDENT ACTIVIST

It's every student's worst nightmare: a school shooting. Yet that's exactly what Emma González experienced on February 14, 2018, in Parkland, Florida. She was lucky. She survived. But seventeen other students and teachers didn't. Afterward, Emma was one of a group of students who decided to campaign for stricter laws on gun control. Because enough was enough. No one wanted this to happen again.

Emma González

BORN: November 11, 1999

NATIONALITY: American

ROLE: Gun-control activist

The Valentine's Day shooting at Marjory Stoneman Douglas High School in Parkland, Florida, was not the first to take place in the United States in 2018. It wasn't even the second. It was the sixth.

In the US, the history of mass shootings at schools is staggering. In 1999, twelve students and one teacher were killed at Columbine High School in Colorado. In 2012, twenty children and six adults were killed at Sandy Hook Elementary School in Connecticut. And these shootings weren't the only ones. During the 20th and 21st centuries, hundreds of other students and teachers have been shot and killed or injured.

Stoneman Douglas students were so outraged that yet another shooting had happened, and that so many of their friends had been killed, that the day after the event, they'd formed the Never Again movement. They didn't want to accept that shootings were part of everyday life. They wanted to stop them.

Three days after the shooting, a student named Emma González gave a powerful speech at a gun-control rally in Florida. In it, she challenged the government to introduce tougher gun laws. The speech went viral. (In four months, it was viewed more than three million times on YouTube.) Now the students were firmly in the spotlight. Three days later, when they traveled to the Florida state capital of Tallahassee to campaign for stricter gun laws, they were on the news again. Donations flooded in to support their March for Our Lives campaign.

The campaign gathered pace. On March 24, 2018, March for Our Lives rallies were held in the US capital and around the country. In Washington, D.C., Emma gave a brief, emotional speech about the events at Stoneman Douglas . . . and then stopped speaking. She stood silently in front of the huge crowd until she'd been on stage for exactly six minutes and twenty seconds—the length of time the shooter was on the loose at her school. Then she told students, *"Fight for your lives before it's someone else's job."*

Emma is just one of the students involved with March for Our Lives. She and many other Stoneman Douglas survivors are working together to challenge gun-control laws. *"We are speaking up for those who don't have anyone listening to them,"* said Emma, *"for those who can't talk about it just yet, and for those who will never speak again."*

Emma González has pointed out to the world that it's often children who lose their lives in mass shootings. So can children also make a difference to the law? Wait and see.

> "We are going to be the kids you read about in textbooks."
>
> EMMA GONZÁLEZ

BE FEARLESS, LIKE EMMA GONZÁLEZ!

Q *It's so unfair. The principal has prohibited students from taking part in an organized protest, even though it's after school. You desperately want to take part, but if you do, you risk getting into a LOT of trouble. What might Emma González do?*

A We don't know for sure what Emma González would do, but as she's so good at standing up for what she believes in, it's likely that she would just go to the protest anyway and risk the backlash. Or perhaps she might decide to go and see the principal and argue so well in favor of her cause that the principal changes their mind . . .

XIUHTEZCATL ROSKE-MARTINEZ

EARTH GUARDIAN

Raised to see nature as something that should always be protected, Xiuhtezcatl Roske-Martinez has been an activist since he was six years old. He has addressed world leaders at the United Nations, given TED talks, and even sued the government for causing climate change. Oh, and he's also a successful author and a hip-hop artist who uses music to remind us that we are ALL Earth's guardians.

NAME: *Xiuhtezcatl Roske-Martinez*

BORN: May 9, 2000

NATIONALITY: American of indigenous Mexican heritage

ROLE: Environmental activist and hip-hop artist

Born in Boulder, Colorado, Xiuhtezcatl (pronounce that "shoo-TEZ-cat") grew up in the Aztec tradition. As a young child, he was taught to see nature as a gift that needs to be taken care of.

Xiuhtezcatl's parents raised him to understand that human greed is having a terrible impact on the planet. In 1992, eight years before he was born, his mother founded Earth Guardians—and he is now its global youth director. The organization's aim is to motivate young people to become leaders in environmental, climate, and social justice movements around the globe.

Xiuhtezcatl was just six when he first took to the stage to tell people about the "sacred planet." He reminded his audience that *"every choice we make is for or against our future."* At nine, he became active in his local community, speaking up about issues such as banning pesticides in parks, charging money for plastic bags, and stopping fracking (a kind of drilling in the earth to release natural gas) in the state of Colorado.

When he was twelve, Xiuhtezcatl was one of the youngest speakers at the United Nations Conference on Sustainable Development in Rio de Janeiro in Brazil—known as Rio+20. The following year, in 2013, President Barack Obama presented him with the United States Volunteer Service Award.

It's not every fifteen-year-old who sues their government, but that's exactly what Xiuhtezcatl did in 2015, when he and twenty other young activists filed a lawsuit against the federal government for "knowingly contributing to climate change." Despite the government's efforts to dismiss it, the lawsuit has won the right to keep proceeding.

Later that year, Xiuhtezcatl was selected to address the General Assembly at the United Nations in New York. That's a pretty big deal, but even more incredibly, he didn't once look at his notes. Instead he addressed the audience directly and said, *"What is at stake right now ... what is in our hands today is the survival of this generation and the continuation of the human race."* At the end of his speech, many of the delegates rose from their seats to show their support.

Music has always been a huge part of Xiuhtezcatl's life. He began writing songs at the age of six and was soon rapping to spread the Earth Guardians' message.

When he was eighteen, Xiuhtezcatl released a hip-hop album called *Break Free*. One of the first songs he wrote for the album, called "Magic," is about what Xiuhtezcatl sees as the reality of our broken world, but also about what communities can do to fight back against it.

Xiuhtezcatl has said that, despite his crazy lifestyle, he's still just a normal teen who likes having fun and doesn't always do the things that he should. But he wants all young people to really think about the power they have to make a difference in the world—and then do something about it.

> ❝ We are fighting for the survival of our generation . . . . We are fighting for kids everywhere. ❞
>
> XIUHTEZCATL ROSKE-MARTINEZ

BE FEARLESS, LIKE XIUHTEZCATL!

Q *You love hanging out with your friends, talking about silly stuff, listening to music, and buying clothes. But part of you feels guilty that you're not more serious and not out there making a difference in the world. What might Xiuhtezcatl Roske-Martinez do?*

A Xiuhtezcatl's parents raised him to be an activist from a really young age, and that certainly doesn't happen to most of us! He'd probably say that of course it's fine to be a normal teen and enjoy being young while we can—but that we can all still find time to think about the stuff that matters. We can't all be superstar change makers, but we're all capable of doing *something*, however big or small, to help make a difference.

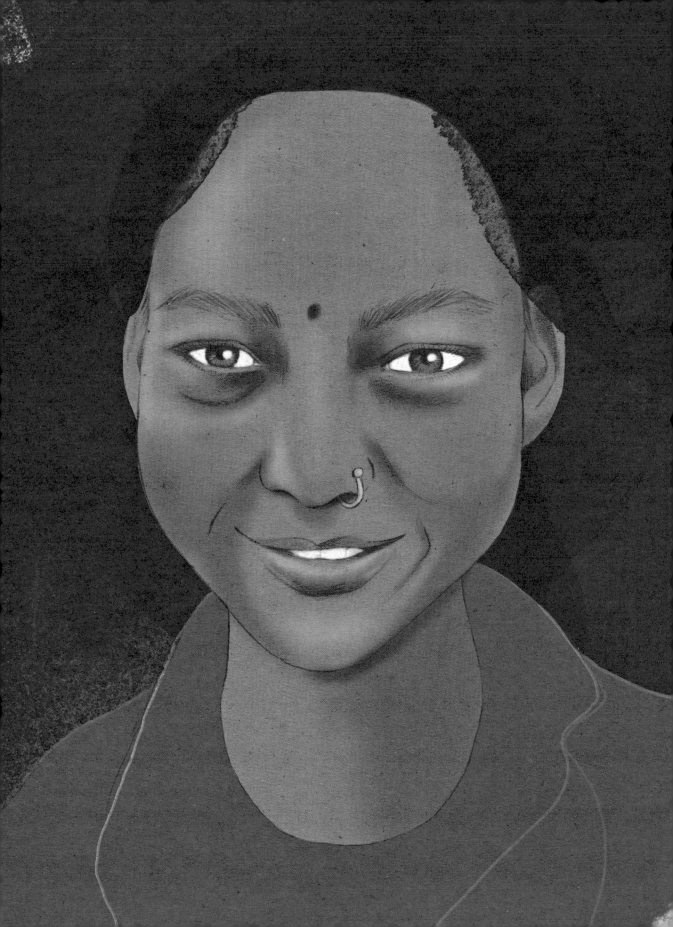

SUNAKALI BUDHA

THE NEPALESE MESSI

High in the mountains of Nepal, food is scarce and life is harsh. After being given the opportunity to be part of a local soccer team, Sunakali Budha showed an incredible ability with the ball. She and her teammates didn't even have a field big enough to practice on, and they often trained in the snow, but their determination carried them all the way to a national soccer tournament—and beyond!

NAME: *Sunakali Budha*

BORN: **2001** (exact date unknown)

NATIONALITY: **Nepalese**

ROLE: **Soccer player**

Sunakali Budha grew up in Mugu, a mountainous region of Nepal that is among the poorest in the world. It is very beautiful, but life is challenging.

Mugu is cut off from civilization, with no real roads. Life is a daily struggle, as food is hard to come by and there is no real access to medical care. There is little education, and it's especially tough for girls—hardly any of them can read, and they are expected to marry once they turn 15.

Sunakali first saw a soccer match when she was ten years old. Then, nearly three years later, Good Neighbors International (GNI)—an organization focusing on development in Nepal—decided to hold a soccer tournament for Nepalese girls. Sunakali was one of fifteen Mugu girls selected to form a team.

Getting anywhere with playing soccer seemed an impossible dream for the girls. They were training at high altitude, and there wasn't even a field large enough for their practice sessions. Meanwhile, their parents disapproved. They expected the girls to focus on their chores. But Sunakali and her teammates were determined. They got up early and often practiced in deep snow.

When it was time for their first competitive match, it was hard for Sunakali and the other girls to convince their parents to let them go. The religious festival Dashain was about to start, and Sunakali's parents thought she would be haunted by evil spirits if she left home. Eventually the girls were allowed to go—on one condition: that they won and did not bring shame on Mugu!

In fact, the girls lost their first match. But soon they had the chance to take part in the national women's soccer championship in the district of Kailali. The girls had to walk for two days to reach the airstrip. It was the first time any of them had left the district, and they had certainly never been on an airplane—or even an oxcart—before.

Incredibly, Team Mugu won their first game. Although the opposing team had more sophisticated skills, the Mugu girls were incredibly fit. Three games later, Sunakali's nimble footwork and impressive goal-scoring ability helped propel the team to victory.

Team Mugu were greeted as heroes at the airstrip, with the locals chanting, *"Sunakali, like Messi!"* The girls rode home on horseback—something women are never normally allowed to do. Villagers lined the route, blessing the players.

Sunakali's extraordinary journey to soccer stardom was captured by the documentary maker Bhojraj Bhat in his award-winning film *Sunakali*. Following the players from the early days of training, it shows the obstacles they had to face. Not only was poverty and their tough homelife an extreme challenge, but they were also fighting against the expectations placed on them as girls.

In reality, day-to-day life has not changed much for Sunakali. She still collects animal food and works hard at her chores. Many of her teammates are now married. But her soccer adventures showed her a glimpse of another world—the possibility of what could be.

BE FEARLESS, LIKE SUNAKALI BUDHA!

Q *You're going on a camping trip, but you're worried you won't enjoy it at all. You're used to a comfy bed, a hot shower, and good food, and you don't like the idea of creepy-crawlies running over your face at night. What might Sunakali Budha do?*

A It's fair to say Sunakali might not be too sympathetic about this one. Sleeping in a cozy sleeping bag? Eating tasty food cooked over a campfire? Luxury! She'd likely tell you to count yourself lucky and embrace the experience. You'll probably love it—and even if you don't, well, your comfy bed will still be there when you get home!

> We've managed to win despite our hardships.
>
> SUNAKALI BUDHA

GRETA THUNBERG

CLIMATE CHANGE WARRIOR

At the age of eleven, Greta became deeply depressed. What was the point of studying for a future when climate change might destroy that future? Then she realized there *was* something she could do. It all began as a solo school strike—but Greta's protest sparked a global movement. She might be small and she might be shy, but she has a huge message for the world: *Now* is the only time to act . . .

NAME: *Greta Thunberg*

BORN: January 3, 2003

NATIONALITY: Swedish

ROLE: Climate-change activist

One Friday in the summer of 2018, fifteen-year-old Greta Thunberg realized enough was enough. For years, climate change had been a "problem" for the world, but she couldn't understand why adults didn't seem to be taking the crisis seriously. So she decided to skip school and sit down outside the Swedish parliament in Stockholm every Friday with a hand-painted banner—*skolstrejk för klimatet* (school strike for the climate). Her demand was that the Swedish government cut carbon emissions to do its part in tackling the world's rising temperatures.

At first Greta was a sad, lonely figure, but gradually she caught the attention of her fellow students, and then the world's media. Inspired by her message to governments across the world—*"You are stealing our future"*—tens of thousands of children began to stage similar school walkouts around the globe. The movement became known as Fridays for Future, and Greta rocketed to fame.

Greta is an unlikely superstar. She has told reporters of how, growing up, she always felt invisible. Painfully shy, she was often bullied at school. In 2015, she was diagnosed with Asperger's syndrome. This means that she finds it difficult to let things go and tends to see things in black and white. She has described her condition as a "gift" though, because it allows her to focus on things without getting distracted, and it makes her determined.

Like many children, Greta watched TV programs about the melting icecaps, the plight of polar bears, and the plastic in our oceans. However, what set her apart from most people was being unable to get those distressing images out of her mind. She fell into depression: she stopped eating, and she only spoke to her family and one teacher.

During this time, Greta began to pressure her parents to change their ways. She persuaded them to give up eating meat and then to get an electric car. Then she convinced them to stop flying—a big move that has affected her mother's international career as a successful opera singer. These steps helped Greta feel her worries were being taken seriously and that she was being listened to. Greta practices what she preaches, too: she never flies and is vegan.

Since having an international profile, Greta has spoken at climate rallies around the world, met many important politicians, and even met with Pope Francis.

In December 2018, she addressed the United Nations Climate Change COP24 Conference in Poland, and in January 2019 and 2020 she attended the World Economic Forum in Davos, Switzerland. Her blunt message—*"Our house is still on fire"*—flew around the world on social media. Greta says she doesn't want people to "hope." She wants them to "panic" because that is the only way change will happen.

In March 2019, Greta was nominated for a Nobel Peace Prize. In May 2019 she appeared on the cover of *Time* magazine, and that December she was named 's the magazine's 2019 Person of the Year. Responding in her Twitter feed to the cover, she simply said, *"Now I am speaking to the world."*

> # "Our house is on fire. I am here to say, our house is on fire.

GRETA THUNBERG

BE FEARLESS, LIKE GRETA THUNBERG!

 Q *You worry all the time about the planet's future—there is doom and gloom on the news, and you hear how plastic is clogging up the world's oceans. When you are out with your friends, you try to avoid anything with plastic packaging. But your friends laugh at you: they say one person can't make any difference! What might Greta Thunberg do?*

A Greta once felt as if there was no point in trying to change anything and that she had no voice. But then she realized that the responsibility belongs to EVERYONE—doing nothing made her feel even more miserable. Some people have mocked Greta, but she'd probably tell you that this never stops her from speaking out. So you could try telling your friends it's their future, too. And if they choose not to listen, at least you can feel satisfied that you are doing your part—*you* are making a difference.

Answer these multiple-choice questions to find out which inspiring youngster you are most like. Make a note of how many As, Bs, Cs, Ds, or Es you score, and then (and *ONLY* then) turn to page 110 for the big reveal.

1. You really want the latest gadget that's all the rage at school, but it's really expensive and you don't have enough money.

a.) Life's too short to let something like money get in the way of your dreams. You'll sell something and get the cash—quick!

b.) Think of all that plastic! The fad will pass and you won't have polluted the planet.

c.) You quiz your parents about why they won't buy you one. Then you can prepare arguments to persuade them why it is a good idea. Or—if they have a point—console yourself about why it must be that way.

d.) If you need money, you'll earn it. A part-time job or chores will get you that cash in no time.

e.) You don't need one—you can invent your own! And if not, you'll have had lots of fun trying.

2. What is the most important quality in a friend?

a.) Someone to have adventures with. Life is for living!

b.) Someone who shares the same values as you.

c.) Someone who listens—you can't really know someone if you don't truly understand them.

d.) Someone who is committed. Friendships don't always just happen. Sometimes you have to work at them.

e.) Someone you can bounce ideas off of.

3. You've recently become vegetarian, but your friends want to go to a restaurant where all the main courses have meat. What do you do?

a.) Well, it's only one evening, and it will be fun. You'll figure out what to do when you get there!

b.) A vegetarian diet really is the best thing for the planet, so you try to convince your friends to be veggie, too. You know a great new place where you could all eat.

c.) You call the restaurant in advance and ask whether they could possibly alter one of the dishes for you.

d.) You're really trying to stick to your new regime, so you'll order something from the menu and just ask for it without the meat. And perhaps have an extra side dish to fill you up.

e.) Invite everyone around to your house instead and say you'll cook.

4. **Your teacher announces that there's going to be an election for a class rep for the school council. What do you do?**

a.) Hmmm, school's not really your thing, and you've got too many other ideas going on in your head. You're happy to let someone else shine in this role.

b.) That sounds like a good forum for making some green changes around school. You'll make sure the new rep knows why the planet is important.

c.) Before you run for election, you ask everyone about their priorities for the school so you can best represent them.

d.) You get organized. You draw up a five-point plan of action and rehearse your debate speech every day. Practice makes perfect!

e.) You're already pretty busy, but when the new rep is elected, you'll offer your help. You've got plenty of creative ideas, after all!

5. **What's your pet peeve?**

a.) Boring classes

b.) Single-use plastic!

c.) Arguments that don't get resolved

d.) Interruptions

e.) Rules

6. **You're nervous about doing a presentation in front of the whole school. How do you prepare?**

a.) You go for a very long run. Exercise always chills you out.

b.) There's a climate emergency. That's what people should be worrying about rather than a silly presentation.

c.) You remember that the audience members are only people. They get nervous sometimes, too, so there's no need to build them up in your mind as something scary.

d.) The best way to control your nerves is with preparation. The more you practice, the better your chances of succeeding and not embarrassing yourself.

e.) You remind yourself that you have some great new ideas that will blow the audience away.

7. **You've been chosen by your drama club for an award. How do you feel?**

a.) It's nice, but you don't tend to get excited about stuff like that. Easy come, easy go!

b.) Happy, but you won't accept it if it's plastic.

c.) How nice to be acknowledged by other people.

d.) Satisfied that your hard work has paid off.

e.) Wonderful. You'll put it next to your other awards.

8. **It's a rainy afternoon and you don't have any plans. What do you do?**

a.) Something high-energy. You're always up for pushing your limits—who cares about the weather . . .

b.) Get outside in nature. It's only rain!

c.) Call a friend for a long catch-up.

d.) Get a headstart on your homework.

e.) Tinker with bits and pieces you have lying around to see what you come up with.

TIMELINE

1972—1985
Samantha Smith

1973
Carlos Acosta

1979
Tawakkol Karman

1991
Thandiwe Chama

1991
Ryan Hreljac

1994
Boyan Slat

1997
Ann Makosinski

1997
Felix Finkbeiner

1999
Sheku
Kanneh-Mason

1929–1945
Anne Frank

1939
Claudette Colvin

1971
Kim Soo-Nyung

1971–1990
Ryan White

approx. 1980
Deng Adut

1981
Jesse Martin

1983–1995
Iqbal Masih

1991
George the Poet

1994
Victoria Arlen

1996–2004
Alexandra Scott

1996
Sonita Alizadeh

1997
Malala Yousafzai

1999
Emma González

2000
Xiuhtezcatl
Roske-Martinez

2001
Sunakali Budha

2003
Greta Thunberg

INDEX